SOCIAL WO

COLORING BOOK

This Book Belongs To:

____

____

COLOR TEST PAGE

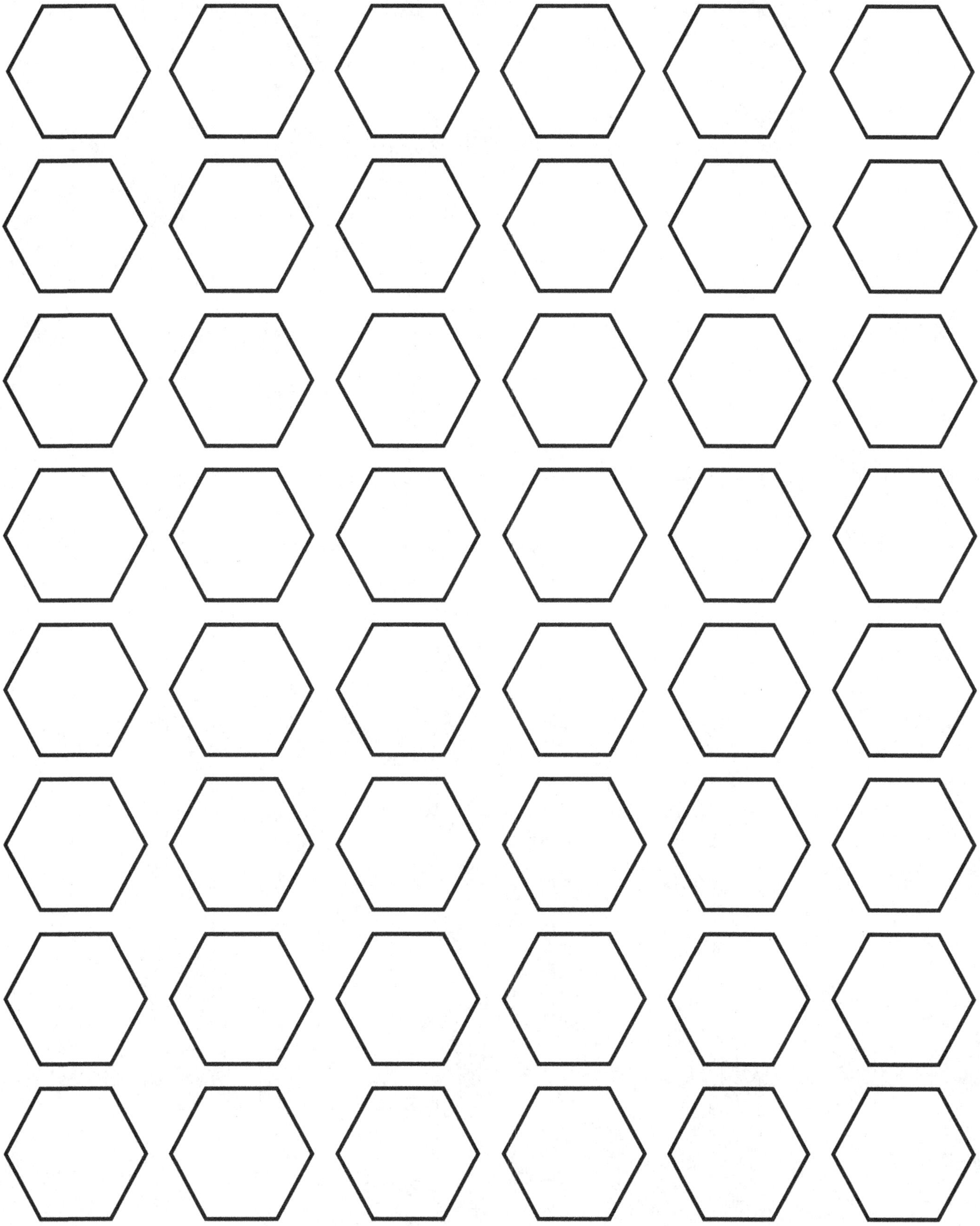

SOCIAL WORKER
LIFE
I make it
LOOK EASY

MAY MY
COFFEE
Be Stronger
THAN MY
CASE LOAD

Documenting
ALL THE THINGS
I WISH I COULD
Forget

I HAVE A
WTF
Is Wrong With People
MOMENT
AT LEAST FOUR TIMES
A DAY

SOCIAL WORKERS
CHANGE THE
WORLD

THIS
SOCIAL WORKER
IS A
freaking
LEGEND

THERE'S A
99%
CHANCE I DON'T
CARE

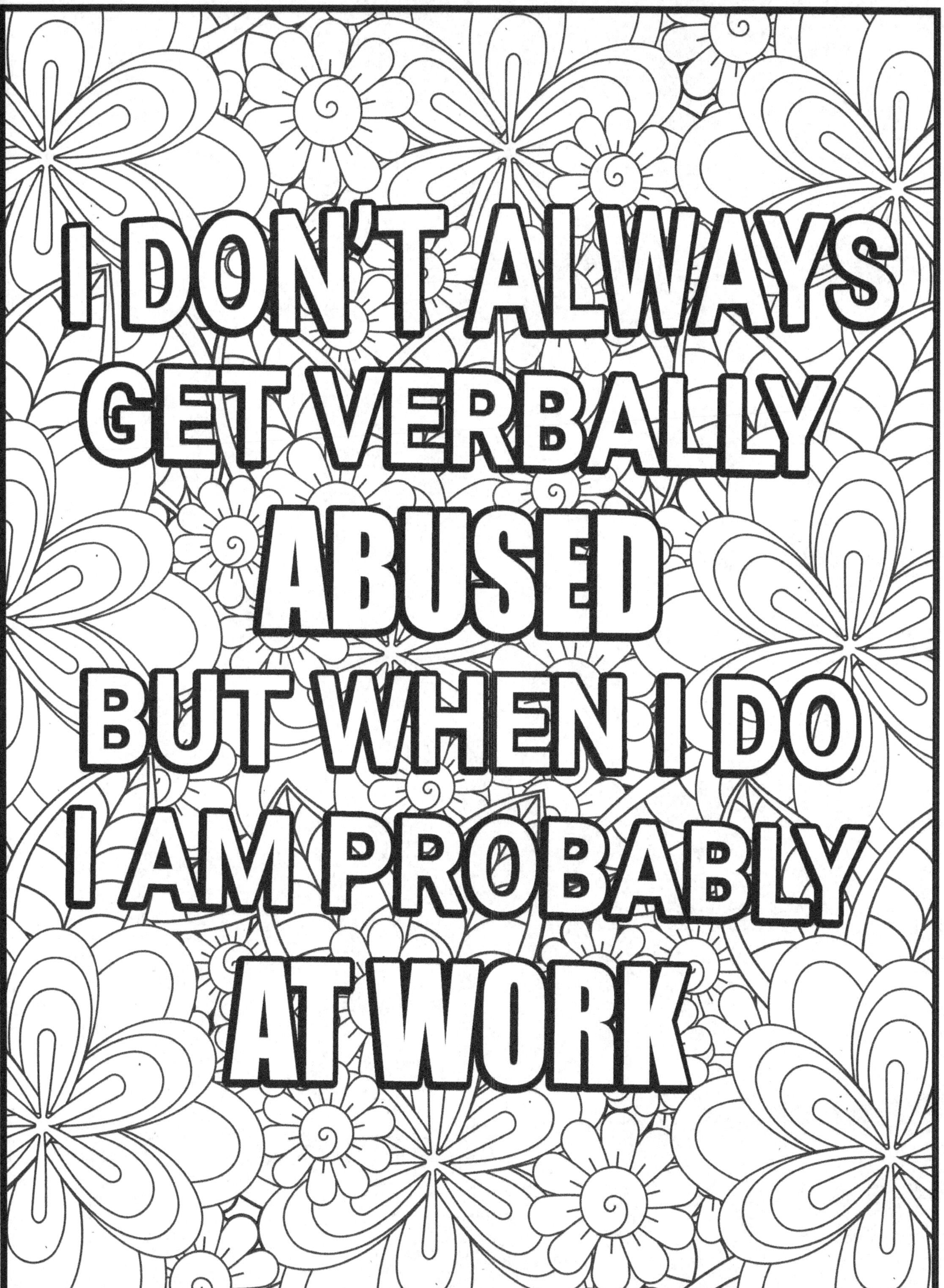
I DON'T ALWAYS
GET VERBALLY
ABUSED
BUT WHEN I DO
I AM PROBABLY
AT WORK

I HATE
Being
BADASS
BUT I AM A
SOCIAL
WORKER
SO I CAN'T
HELP IT

I GAVE UP
My Life
TO LEARN
HOW TO
Save Yours

THIS
SOCIAL
WORKER
NEEDS A
Six Months
VACATION
Twice a Year

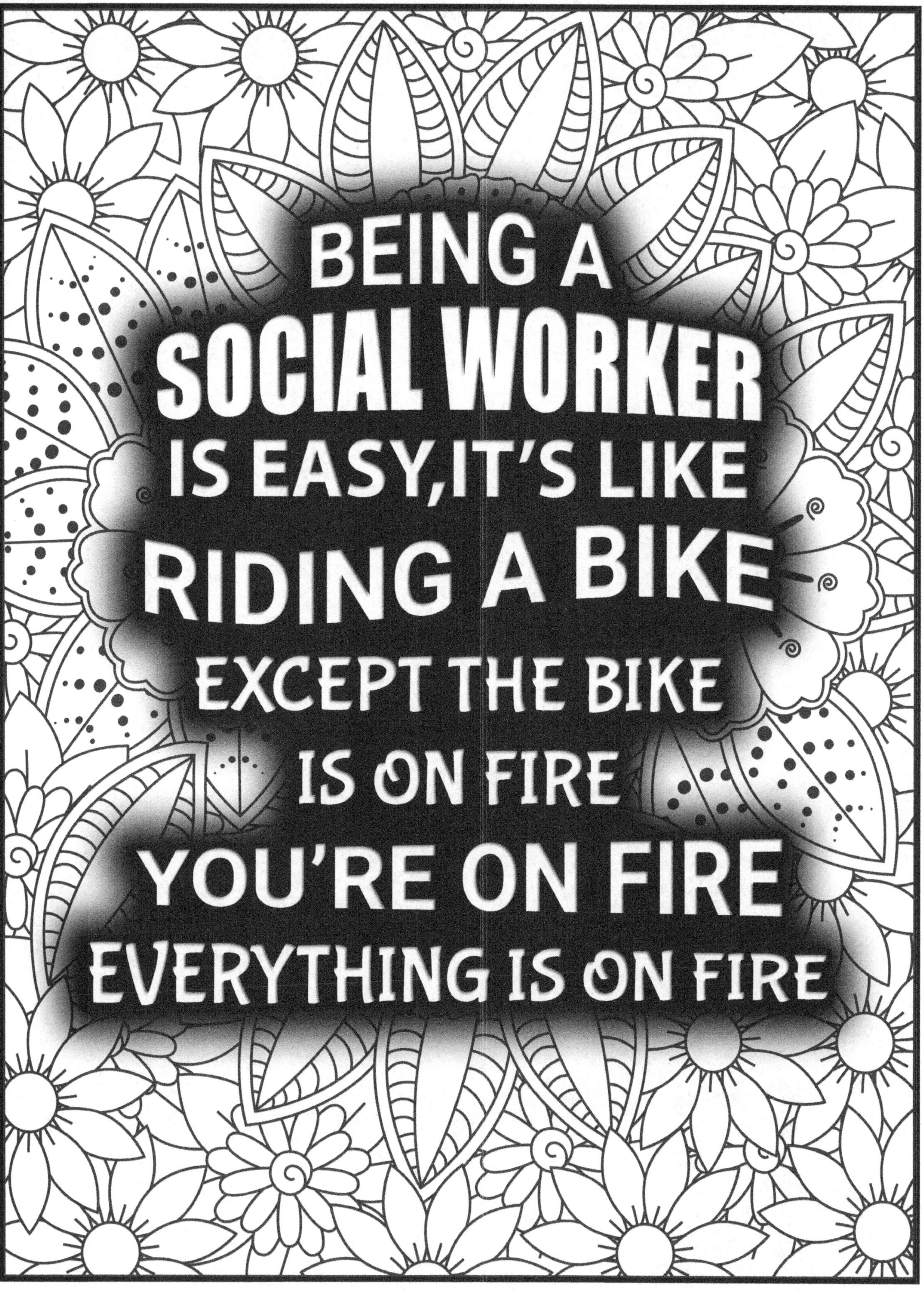
BEING A
SOCIAL WORKER
IS EASY, IT'S LIKE
RIDING A BIKE
EXCEPT THE BIKE
IS ON FIRE
YOU'RE ON FIRE
EVERYTHING IS ON FIRE

I'M NOT
JUDGING
I'M
ASSESSING

SOCIAL WORKER
LLAMA
AIN'T GOT TIME
FOR YOUR
DRAMA

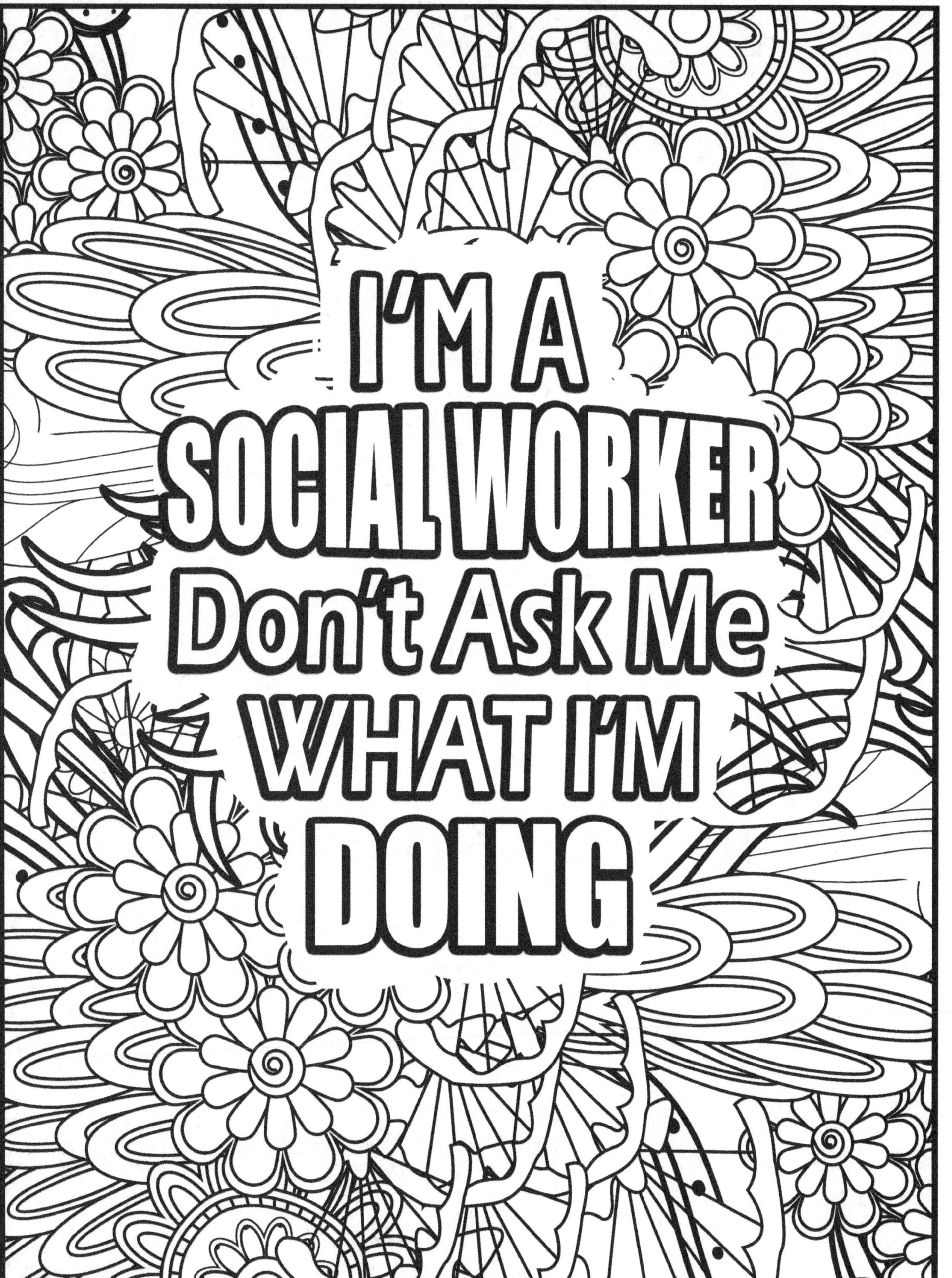
I'M A
SOCIAL WORKER
Don't Ask Me
WHAT I'M
DOING

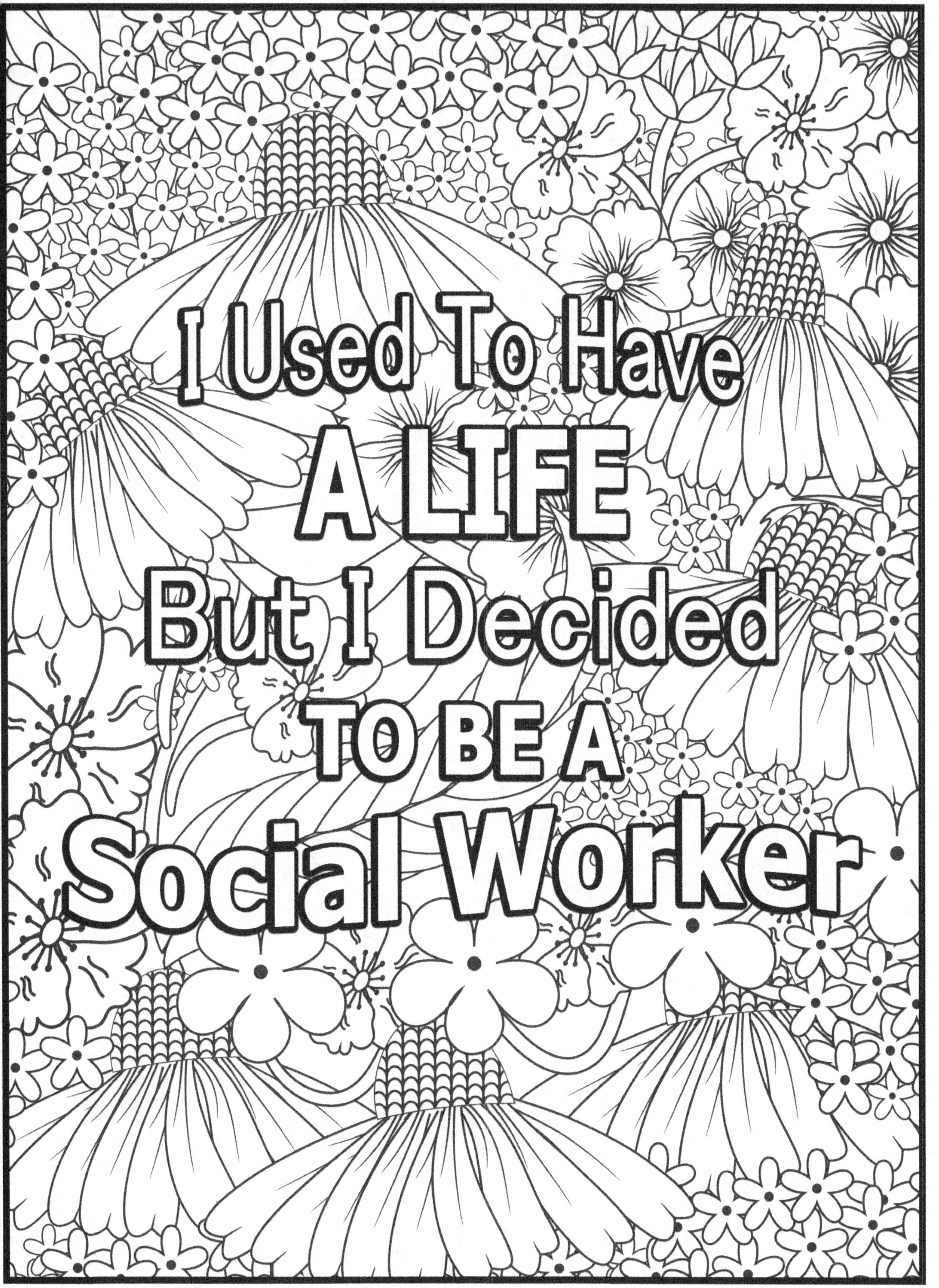
I Used To Have
A LIFE
But I Decided
TO BE A
Social Worker

BEING A
SOCIAL
WORKER
IS A
WORK
OF
HEART

DON'T MAKE ME
USE MY
SOCIAL
WORKER
VOICE

No Matter
HOW HARD
Life Gets
AT LEAST YOU ARE A
SOCIAL WORKER

THIS
SOCIAL
WORKER
IS OFF
DUTY

Made in United States
North Haven, CT
08 December 2024

62041771R00026